Red
Animals

Melissa Stewart

Enslow Elementary

an imprint of

Enslow Publishers, Inc.
40 Industrial Road
Box 398
Berkeley Heights, NJ 07922
USA

http://www.enslow.com

S

Enslow Elementary, an imprint of Enslow Publishers, Inc.
Enslow Elementary® is a registered trademark of Enslow Publishers, Inc.

Library of Congress Cataloging-in-Publication Data
Stewart, Melissa.
    Red animals / Melissa Stewart.
        p. cm. — (All about a rainbow of animals)
    Includes bibliographical references and index.
    Summary: "Introduces pre-readers to simple concepts about red animals using short sentences and repetition of
words"—Provided by publisher.
    ISBN 978-0-7660-3995-7 (alk. paper)
    1. Animals—Color—Juvenile literature. 2. Red—Juvenile literature. I. Title.
    QL767.S7445 2012
    590—dc23
                                    2011027247
Future editions:
Paperback ISBN 978-1-4644-0042-1
ePUB ISBN 978-1-4645-0949-0
PDF ISBN 978-1-4645-0949-7

Printed in the United States of America
012012 The HF Group, North Manchester, IN
10 9 8 7 6 5 4 3 2 1

To Our Readers: We have done our best to make sure all Internet Addresses in this book were active and appropr
when we went to press. However, the author and the publisher have no control over and assume no liability for the
material available on those Internet sites or on other Web sites they may link to. Any comments or suggestions can
sent by e-mail to comments@enslow.com or to the address on the back cover.

Photo Credits: © 2011 Photos.com, a division of Getty Images, pp. 3 (spider), 10, 20; © iStockphoto.com/Alfred
Maiquez, pp. 1, 12; Shutterstock.com, pp. 3 (sea star, spider), 4, 6, 8, 14, 16, 18.

Cover Photo: Shutterstock.com

Note to Parents and Teachers

Help pre-readers get a jumpstart on reading. These lively stories introduce simple concepts with repetition of
words and short simple sentences. Photos and illustrations fill the pages with color and effectively enhance the
text. Free Educator Guides are available for this series at www.enslow.com. Search for the *All About a Rainbow
of Animals* series name.

Contents

Words to Know

crab   sea star   spider

red bird

red snake

red ladybug

red spider

red frog

red fish

red crab

red sea star

monkey with a red face

red animals

Read More

Jenkins, Steve. *Living Color.* Boston: Houghton Mifflin, 2007.

Whitehouse, Patricia. *Colors We Eat: Red Foods.* Chicago: Heinemann, 2004.

Web Sites

Animal Colors
http://www.highlightskids.com/Science/Stories/SS1000_
animalColors.asp

Animal Printable Coloring Pages
http://thecoloringspot.com/animals-coloring-pages/

Index

Guided Reading Level: A
Guided Reading Leveling System is based on the guidelines
recommended by Fountas and Pinnell.

Word Count: 24